"Habit is overcome by Habit"

Erasmus

"Time is one of the only things you cannot inherit, steal, or borrow."

The Habit Changing Handbook

Acknowledgements

Authors

Richard Winterbourne BABCP
Daniel Carey MCMI

Cover Art

Cover photo by Uwe Scholz
"Stair case study house 02"
Used with the kind permission of the architect,
Gerd Streng BDA www.gerdstreng.de

Published October 2018

"A Habit is only a Habit until you observe it,
then it's a choice"

Contents

"Never allow waiting to become a habit.
Live your dreams and take risks.
Life is happening now."

1. Introductions.

Hi. I'm Hardy Grey

And I'm Mrs Grey – Alice.

'We just wanted to say hello and welcome you to our habit changing handbook, well it's your book now of course. It has been written to help you learn about, control and change your habits, especially procrastination!'

'I couldn't have put it better myself Alice. In this habit changing handbook we will show you how to rid yourself of negative habits, the kind of habits that your subconscious keeps you a slave to and we will also show you how to create positive habits to put in their place and stop procrastinating. How cool is that?'

'Perfectly put Mr Grey, the book is so simple that even you can follow it and it's easy to carry around. Not much in the way of "psycho-babble", just straight forward logical stuff. Once you've got it, you've got it! Brilliant!'

Cleverley though it's still based on proven therapeutic techniques and the route shown will always work if you, the reader, follow the guidelines of the book. It has worked for loads of people, so it can work for you. If you get stuck we are here to help, well at least I am"

'Do you even know just how much control you actually have over your life and your destiny?

Have you ever wondered why some people just seem to have worked it all out?

That's the point of this book to give you back control, and we both just love it!'

Look to the future you deserve and long for - it's here for the taking.

'The question is then, how are you going to do this?'

'Let me explain...'

'Oh, don't worry Alice I wouldn't get in your way, you go ahead'

'Thank you, Hardy, ...

The structure of the brain works in particular ways and we know that.

The way forward for changing your habits is working with the brain's strengths and weaknesses.

Think of me as the Strength and Hardy as... well you get the idea.

The brain works on your repeated behaviours that then become your habits. It relies on building structures around your habits to support them. In this book we will show you how this works and how the way that your habits are supported is the key to change. It really is simple, once you know how'

'We both know, as do you that you really want to sort out your managing of your time which is why you bought this book, right?

But have you thought why you want to change?

You need to get that pretty clear in your head...'

'What is the point?

Why will it help?

What's in it for me?'

'When Hardy stopped smoking the benefit was pretty obvious, apart from smelling a whole lot better obviously it impacted on his health, our wealth and it stopped me being constantly left on my own in pubs whilst he went outside to smoke with his other smoking buddies. So, we spent more time together, ok so not all good then'

Oh, very funny!

'I know... anyhow most of our habits unfortunately are not that black and white however and the gains and losses can be a bit more smudged. For example, creating a good habit of getting up early and doing some exercise every day seems like a win-win situation, what's to consider?

'Do you remember when I first tried that?

'How can I forget'

'Well it makes sense that when I was getting up earlier I had to go to bed earlier, makes sense right? If I hadn't there was no way that I would have kept that up.'

'I get that, but it also impacted on me and my evenings, you wanted to eat earlier, go to bed earlier, do everything earlier, if you know what I mean, it wasn't just about you, but you didn't consider that did you?'

'Frankly? no.'

'So, it's important then to look at everything that your change could impact?

'Sounds like a perfect recipe for more time wasting to me"

Time to stop babbling and leave the reader to get on with it...

We hope you enjoy the journey, just remember, we believe in you!'

2. Knowing 'Why' you want to change.

To stop procrastinating something has to change. Goals and clarity are crucial to making the right decision for change and goal setting is an integral part of the habit changing process to help you stop procrastinating.

Making the right decision will impact greatly on your success in this book. Therefore, to help you in making the decision to stop procrastinating…

You have to know your 'why'!

WHY do you want to stop procrastinating?

Looking at your goals and what you want to achieve, is more important than picking a habit to change. Figure out what you want to be different in your life and change the habits that give you that goal.

Once your goal is clear and you know which habit you want to tackle or create, this becomes your PRIMARY HABIT, that is, where the focus for change will be.

Now we know the primary habit – procrastinating, is what you want to change you need to figure out what allows your procrastination habit it to exist.

There are 'things' that are supporting that habit, and whatever they are, they need to be replaced by something else that helps build your new habit, i.e. not procrastinating any more. Those 'somethings' are known as "supporting habits" and there are two types – "Feeder Habits" and "Builder Habits". We will go into more detail on feeder and builder habits in chapters 6 and 7

Which is where the fun starts - but first you need to understand what habits are and the process for changing them. Changing habits is about changing a structure upon which behaviour is built.

It does take a little work, a little focus and a smattering of determination, but when you know your 'why', when you know the reason and the benefits both in the short and the long term changing your habits forever will give you control and the life that you want.

This habit changing handbook explains what a Habit is, why we have them and why sometimes they can seem impossible to break or create new habits.

The power of a strongly ingrained habit can seem overwhelming, so this book shows you the process of how to capture that power and turn the habit from negative to positive.

Our brains love habits and fights hard to keep them, the process we are covering in this book tricks the brain into focusing on new and positive habits whilst rejecting old and negative habits. After a short while your brain will begin not only to accept the small changes but also to expect and crave the changes of behaviour that you want and have tasked yourself.

This is a crucial part of teaching yourself to expect and believe in your own ability to change and a growing belief in permanent change and success. It is that permanent change that we are after, which is why this habit changing process works as well as it does.

The Habit Changing Handbook

Through the process of identifying and then changing small 'feeder' or 'builder' habits - those that support a 'primary' habit you discover how easy it is to either take away the foundations of a negative habit or build foundations of a positive habit for permanent change. (See pages 25 to 31 for more on this)

Imagine a tower of "Jenga" blocks. On top of that tower is your primary habit (the one you really want to change) However, with all the pieces in place the tower is strong, and your habit won't budge.

But if you start to take away some of the blocks, which in this example are the supporting habits, the tower will become weaker, take away too many and the tower will come crashing down. Therefore, if the habit that you want to change has no supporting structure - it cannot exist.

 Now imagine building a new tower out of better supporting blocks, i.e. "builder habits" to support the new primary habit you have decided on – no more procrastinating and actually "getting stuff done" instead of previously "putting stuff off"

Part of the process of change is writing about your experience of what you are changing and how you are changing it. We will go into more detail on this later. In the meantime, think on the following…

Q: What creates a habit in the first place?
A: Repeated behaviour.

Q: So, to change your habits you need…?
A: New repeated behaviour from you!

So, let's begin… "Today we change our future"

3. What is a Habit?

Simply put, a habit is a repeated behaviour to the point where it becomes subconscious or without conscious thinking. It can be described as a fixed way of thinking or feeling which is taken from a repeated experience.

Often habits are created without the person being aware of it because we don't over think boring routine, thoughts or tasks. Habits become imprinted in our brains and are primarily stored in the part of our brains named the Basal Ganglia.

Take for example a simple practice that is repeated by us all and the way in which we do it becomes a very personal habit - cleaning our teeth.

It is a process and behaviour that we repeat, once, twice or more times a day, but when was the last time you thought about which side of your mouth you start brushing first? You don't. You just start, the same way you do EVERY time.

If you don't believe me, try it.

Go to your bathroom and deliberately clean your teeth in a completely different way and see how it feels? Awkward and even a little weird.

The repeated behaviour is what the brain expects.

Change the experience and the brain wonders what is going on. At some point in your life you made the decision which way you clean your teeth, EVERY time, but I bet you don't remember when and why you did? -That's Habit!

Can you imagine then how many habits we have that we are not conscious of?

How many decisions we have made about the way that we live every day, decisions we never question. We just accept them as a part of us, even if we bother to think about it.

Take a moment, grab a piece of paper and write down ten habits that you are aware of, not necessarily bad ones, but everyday ones that go by unnoticed, it's not an easy task but see if you can recognise a few.

Here are a few examples to get you thinking...

- Which sock, or shoe do you always put on first?
- Do you always have tea at the same time of the morning?
- Which shoelaces do you tie first?
- Are you aware how often you check your phone?
- Do you eat whether you are hungry or not?

Each of these examples and of course some of your very own habits are very deep routed and in themselves are completely harmless.

The awareness of habits and what they are, is an important step in understanding to beating, changing or creating them. Knowledge is power.

Think for a moment about a habit that you have that perhaps you would like to change or get rid of completely a habit that you know impacts on your life or possibly wellbeing?

Imagine then telling yourself in this moment that you will never indulge in that habit again, ever, as in the rest of your life, never again.

How does that feel?

Initially it can feel pretty good, even uplifting.

Now think about how it would feel to never have that sense of satisfaction or release when you indulge in that habit, not so uplifting?

If you recoil or panic quietly at the realistic thought of never enjoying that habit again, then you know the power of habit and the true meaning of the word.

> The fixidity of a habit in generally in direct
> proportion to its absurdity
> (Proust)

4. Why do we have Habits?

The science can be summed up easily, if you don't want to get too clever and for our purposes we don't, let's keep it simple.

Habits, as we have said are stored in the wonderfully named and hugely versatile part of the brain called the Basal Ganglia. The name is of no importance, I just like it.

This cluster of Neurons based deep within the brain has a great number and variety of functions.

These include voluntary movement, cognition and eye movement. I did tell you it was versatile.

However, there is a great deal of growing evidence that along with habit learning when there is a dysfunction in the Basal Ganglia (There I said it again) this can be where we learn Obsessive Compulsive Disorder (OCD) It is also be where the neurological pathway that leads to addiction and a central role in reward learning is based. Narcotics such as Heroin and Cocaine rely on this pathway.

All of this makes the Basal Ganglia of great interest to anyone wanting to understand habits. Its' part of being Human.

But why? It's easy to say that it's just the way that we function but we are evolving beings, so what do we gain from having habits? Surely there must be a reason?

One theory goes like this;

The more routine, basic stuff that our brain can store as repetitive memory or habit the less it has to work. So, when we have a habit which is sub conscious, i.e. the brain doesn't have to think about it, the less the brain has to work. It is therefore to the brains advantage to create as many habits as it can so that it works as little as possible. (sounds like someone I know)

The reason for this is, so the argument goes is that the less work the brain has to do, the smaller and more compact it can be. The smaller the brain, the smaller the head. This leads to more mothers and babies surviving child birth. This in turn makes us as a human race more populous and therefore more successful.

There you have it, it is all to do with evolution! Think Charles Darwin.

It's no wonder then that breaking habits can be so incredibly hard to do, we are battling with the very forces of evolution and that's a lot to face up to when your brain is whispering in your ear, "Go on, you know you want to, one more won't hurt you can always stop tomorrow?"

So, the drive to couch surf and watch another box set whilst devouring Hagen Das ice cream washed down with some fizz, rather than make the effort to change and get an early night and have an apple is millions of years in the making! (maybe that's just me but you get the idea)

It is of course not that simple and the reality is we DO have a choice in what we do, it's just a lot easier to give in rather than change.

If you have ever tried to change a habit, do you notice that its sometimes really difficult to focus long enough to do it? You keep getting distracted? That is the brain pushing you back into the same old rut and like most ruts it can be extremely difficult to get out of. The rut of habit.

Just imagine then that by making a choice to change and using the technique in this book, you can use all of that negative power to create a positive good habit and rid yourself of the self- destructing ones...

You can create your own personal evolution.

5. What is a negative habit and how do we recognise it?

That seems like an obvious question, which should have an obvious answer, but that is often not the case.

In simple terms a negative habit is a habit that has a negative impact on you, your surroundings, your loved ones or for that matter any effect on your goals in life.

It's obvious when you write it or read it but often some of our most destructive habits we either choose to ignore or not recognise them as negative at all or see the damage that they do.

Recognition therefore of your Primary negative habit, the one you want to change, is essential. Shining a light on it and looking objectively and honestly takes courage but then, you knew that when you bought this book.

What may be harder to see at first... are all of the small, almost invisible habits (feeder habits) that support or allow your obvious Primary habit to exist.

For example,

One of the most common things about negative habits is that we either don't recognize it as negative or we dress it up in our own minds as something positive or we just choose to ignore it.

So, let's look at something that we will all recognize either from ourselves or from someone that we know.

Staying up late every night into the early hours on social media or catching up with your latest box series, you should not be surprised if you are too tired to function well the next day. The Negative habit is staying up too late, but the supporting or feeder habits are looking at TV or staying on social media.

Not getting enough sleep and the negative consequences for you are that you are possibly too tired and grumpy and then possibly unable to think or work properly the next day. For those around you, they have to deal with a bear with a sore head.

In this particular case you may not recognize going to bed late and not getting enough sleep as a negative habit because you have justified it in your own mind as chilling out before the drudgery of work again the next day, important down time, perhaps the one time of day you have to relax.

It is very likely that you see it as positive? But the true consequences may be far more negative over time than you think?

Let's look at both sides... As a quick exercise, swap these comments around into the either positive or negative columns. Start with the negative finish with the positive.

Negative	← Which column →	Positive
	Own time and space	
	Tired the next day	
	Impact on your work/job	
	Less receptive to others needs	

Another example might be....

Busying yourself...

- running around doing chores and favours for others
- writing out list after list, even having a list of lists!
- preparing and polishing what you need to do.
- making sure that everything is perfectly in place before you actually start what you really need to do

Frequently however you never get around to do the task that you have set yourself because of course the time is never quite right, the list never quite honed enough and there is always something to do that is just too important first.

After all, how can you not answer the phone to your mum or your best friend.

They may need you.

Any excuse not to do the task.

THAT'S PROCRASTINATION!

You may argue that it is better to be ultra-ready and organised before starting what you need to do and that could be seen as positive. However, as the story goes, if you wait for the right time to do something, that time will never come. If you put it off until tomorrow, as you did yesterday, nothing will ever happen or change. That's a very common and big negative habit.

If you recognise that in yourself and let's face it most of us will, take a moment to think about some of your very favourite excuses, sorry very important reasons, that you don't get that task done.

Better still - grab a pen or pencil and jot them down.

For example;

- Getting it right
- Never getting it done
- Building up negativity around it
- Feeling bad about yourself

Whatever your primary habit is, however deeply engrained it may be, understanding what it is and how it impacts on you is essential before you can change it. Once you have recognised it and have accepted it you can begin to make a strategy to change it. Outwit your old habits, trick your brain and prove once and for all you can teach an old brain, new tricks.

Focus now on how different your life will be without that negativity holding you back, don't dwell on the past but rather focus on the future - look forward.

This is the moment then, there is no hiding from it, if you want to change this is the way forward.

6. Preparing to change

Let's take a moment then to reflect on this habit you want to change – to stop procrastinating.

This is the 'Primary Habit'

Think about what it will mean to you not to have it, close your eyes and imagine how that will feel.

importance alert!

If you close your eyes and think how life will be without your negative Primary Habit or how life will be with your new shiny positive one and it doesn't really change your life much and frankly you are just not feeling it?

It is essential that this change will be great enough for you to really want to succeed. If it's not moving you before you start, then this is going nowhere. Passion for change must be matched with passion for the result.

So, look again at your Primary Habit, how much do you want to change it? If the answer is not...

"OMG - YES PLEASE - IT HAS TO GO, AND I CAN'T WAIT!!!!"

...then look for one that does make you feel like that - go no further until you want to scream those words.

So now you have made that decision to change and stop procrastinating any more, this is how you are going to get rid of your negative procrastination habit... you are going to work on those supporting habits that were mentioned previously.

You are going to replace those negative feeder habits with positive builder habits that will support your new primary habit- being proactive instead of procrastinating.

Let's get this out there... replacing your procrastination habit with being proactive is not going to happen overnight – to work properly this process will take a few weeks. The process will take some time and effort on your part, quite a lot of focus and buckets of determination. By paying attention to and using the step by step process in this habit changing handbook over the next few weeks, you will make this process as easy as possible for yourself.

"28 days later"

The time you are going to invest (in yourself) is only 28 days, that's just four weeks.

It may seem like a long time but is it really?

- Remember as a child how quickly the summer holidays went?
- As an adult, doesn't your two-week holiday seem to be over too quickly?
- Suddenly Christmas is here!
- "Where did this year go?"
- "Doesn't time fly!"

The time will pass quickly, and you WILL change if you use the process properly.

The reason it takes four weeks is because you are re-training your brain.

You will be creating a new reality for yourself which we assume you will want that those new habits to be permanent.

The new foundations of any change require time to settle.

Don't be impatient with yourself, the handbook or the process.

The process will work if you work the process!

Now that we've covered the process, let's take a look at these "feeder habits"

7. What is a Feeder Habit?

A 'Feeder Habit' is a small sometimes insignificant supporting habit that enables your bigger, main 'Primary Habit' to exist. In fact, you could look at it as though it is a co-conspirator.

Feeder Habits prop-up and support your main habit by letting it flourish. A Feeder Habit in itself is not necessarily bad but, just like an easily influenced teenager in a group or gang of like-minded individuals, it will allow the leader or Primary Habit to do things it could never normally do alone.

Our aim then is to take away all of this bad support, kick away the props and distract the individual gang members away one at a time until nothing remains of the Feeder Habits, the tower has collapsed, and the Primary Habit lies broken on the ground.

Let's take your Primary Habit of procrastination as an example.

What Feeder Habits do you have that could be supporting it?

If, for you, Procrastination is about putting things off to a later date then these examples below may be small Feeder Habits that contribute to your procrastination habit and preventing you from doing what you should be doing.

1. Being distracted, spending too much time on social media?

2. Vegetating on the couch, maybe watching too much TV?

3. Going late to bed and getting up late in the morning?

These are just three simple examples; Can you think of anymore more that are more applicable to you?

8. Creating Good Habits through Builder Habits

We have explored what a negative habit is, and we have ventured into why we have them, well let's turn that on its head.

You may have picked up this book thinking I don't really have any habits I want to get rid of but there are plenty I would like to have?

How do I create, grow, nurture and keep a good and positive habit?

As we now know, habits are repeated behaviours that we continue to do until they become subconscious and that is the point that they become fully fledged habits.

So, to create a new and positive habit we have to do the very opposite to ridding ourselves of a negative habit, we have to build the foundations of a new one.

Let's explain.

Take an example of wanting to do more exercise? That seems like a good and positive habit to have but how do I start?

- Put some running shoes on and hit the streets?
- Join the local gym or swimming pool?
- Perhaps go to some classes?

All of the above idea's are great of and it's what millions of us do whenever we get the idea that something needs to change, for some that's the answer.

However, now ask yourself this...

How often have I started to do something from the list above only to stop a few days/ weeks /months later? How many people do I know that have done the same thing?

If it makes you feel better that is what the majority of us do. We are full of good intentions but weak when it comes to commitment. Welcome to the human race!

The reason we stop is because we don't look at the whole picture. We may start at the gym or go to classes but all the rest of our habits that have supported a non-active lifestyle are still in place!

In other words, you are trying to create a new and positive habit with the Feeder Habits of a negative lifestyle.

In this diagram, you can see the difficulty in trying to create something new using old, outdated and negative habit material.

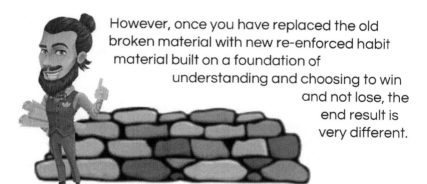

However, once you have replaced the old broken material with new re-enforced habit material built on a foundation of understanding and choosing to win and not lose, the end result is very different.

The lesson here therefore is, to create a new and positive habit we have to do the very opposite to ridding ourselves of a negative habit, we have to build the foundations of a new one.

Creating builder habits offers us a chance to build something permanent and strong. The habit becomes resilient because you have underpinned your new habit with supporting behaviours.

Once you have selected your goal and have your builder habits in place you are ready to move on to the next stage!

This is where the magic starts to happen, where you start to understand and identify those builder habits.

This is it guys" – The next stage – identifying the negative feeder habits that are holding up and supporting that bad primary habit you want to change.

As you can see in this diagram, the main or primary habit in the centre is being fed by bad or negative "Feeder" habits. Each Feeder habit is having a negative effect on your goal, i.e. it is actually supporting no change for the better – holding you back.

So, it's fairly obvious what we need to do once we identify what those Feeder habits are – replace them with positive Builder habits – and therefore helping the new and improved good positive primary habit that you want to achieve in the centre.

Here, the new positive Primary habit is being supported by good positive builder habits

You can see in these two comparisons that the builder habits replace the feeder habits therefore not leaving room for the old habits to return.

Let's take a real-world example; a goal to "get fitter".

"Getting Fitter "is the primary habit that for the sake of the exercise we are going to use. It is one that many of us suffer from at one point or another in our lives.

"Getting fitter" is the goal and is written as the primary habit in the middle box.

What do you think the "feeder habits" are in this "getting fitter" example?

- Too many biscuits and cakes?
- Binge watching box sets till the early hours?
- Not exercising enough?
- Social media Vs going to the Gym?

What builder habits could you replace your feeder habits with?

- Cutting down on alcohol
- Going to bed earlier and sleeping better?
- Checking your diet? Less sugary foods?
- Manage your time better – Less social media?

Combining the above two illustrations shows how the builder habits are replacing the feeder habits over the coming weeks.

The end result is that the old bad habit is now replaced by a new good habit being supported by those new builder habits.

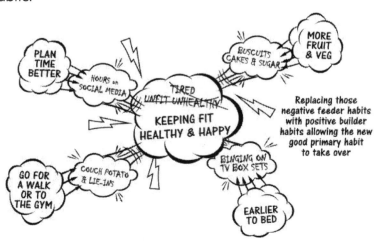

When you start your process. we recommend you take a blank sheet of paper or one of our downloadable templates and start mapping this out for yourself.

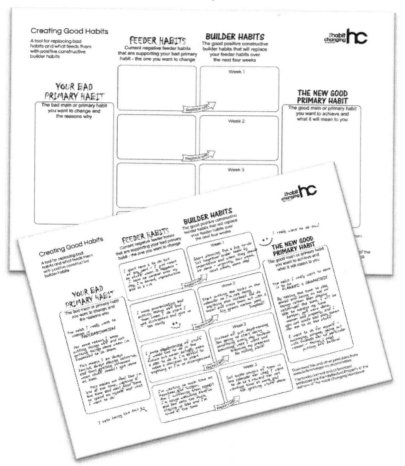

There's a larger version of this in the appendix.

Once you have selected your goal and have your builder habits in place you are ready to move on to the next stage!

You can download our blank templates from bit.ly/hcprintables

9. The Process of Creating Good Habits

Introducing the four-week process

In this key part of the process it is important that each of these feeder or builder habits are clear in your own mind as these will determine the outcome of your journey.

The process

At the beginning of week one you will begin to change the feeder habits and introduce the builder habits.

In the example the habits in week one (feeder habit going to bed late and not getting up early) and your (builder habits are 'going to bed by 11pm and getting up by 7am).

So that is all you change. at no time are you directly addressing your problem with Procrastination.

The achievement of those goals for week 1 is all you have to do. That's it!

At the end of week 1 your brain will begin to accept change in your habits and behaviours are slowly and most importantly your brain is beginning to recognize and accept not only this specific change but also the concept of change.

Running alongside this is the building sense of self belief and this is an important part of change. Just stick to this simple step by step guide and you will see change.

At the beginning of week 2 the example shows that we are working on feeder habit 2 and builder habit 2.

Again, as in week 1 you can now concentrate on these two new dimensions in your behaviour but not forgetting your week 1 commitment.

By the end of week 2 your patterns of behaviour change, and habit readjustment should be becoming very obvious. You have changed 2 negative habits and created 2 new positive ones.

The sense of self belief will become a driving force in its own right and will propel you forward for weeks 3 and 4.

The reason that this will work for you is because you are taking each step at a time and focusing on it without leaving the vacuum for slipping backwards. Concentrating on each individual week and not being tempted to jump forward or to skip a step is essential and will prove to be a concrete foundation for change. Be patient, be changed.

Remember, if you shortcut the process, your brain will shortcut the result.

Setting goals takes some careful consideration. If the goal is too much or too high, failure to reach it becomes almost inevitable.

However, if the goal is not high enough to challenge you or at least keep your attention it becomes irrelevant and again failure is pretty much inevitable.

So how then do we reach a balance?

It's always about the why?

Having a goal for a goal's sake is ok but unless you have a reason for doing it the goal becomes much harder to achieve.

Take for example getting up at 4am on a Sunday morning.

Just because you decide it is what you are going to do it may be a little trickier if you have no specific gain.

If, however you were getting up because you were passionate about sunrises or to hear the birds sing or even because you were leaving to go on holiday, then it becomes a whole new ball game.

You have a why and the stronger it is the easier the goal becomes.

So, let's look at why you may want to change or create a habit.

If for example your goal is to stop procrastinating what might be your reasons for that goal?

- Get stuff done?
- Achieve greater success in my business
- Feel less stressed and more confident?

These are just three possible "Why's". How about thinking of three more that are more applicable and personal to you?

All of us whilst trying to change or create habits will have stronger and weaker days, that is because we are human and as we have already discovered there is a lot of pressure from our brain NOT to change.

When looking for your "Why" it is best to take a while to imagine and envisage how different your life will be once your new lifestyle kicks in. Take time to feel the difference and make sure that you want it. The strength of your 'Why' is crucial - That's why you start with it.

Most failures come from people who have the habit of making excuses

(Unknown)

10. Setting goals that you will achieve

To have a clear objective, a clear goal, a vision of how different you are going to be once you have beaten this habit is an essential part of the journey. You wouldn't get on a bus or a plane unless you knew the final destination - so why would you now on one of the most important journeys that you will ever take? The journey to where, what and who you want to be.

This is a learning process, a lesson that will stay with you, one that you can use again and again. The most important part is that you learn how to change yourself, you learn to take back control, you learn that you can make choices.

So, when you set your goal, your target, remember that this is the first one that you will do so make it important but achievable, life changing but not clearly out of reach in fifty-six days.

For example, if you said:

"I am going to lose 42lbs, get fit, find a partner, get married and make my first million all within four weeks"

… that's a bit "too fluffy" and you are probably aiming too high.

However maybe something more detailed and realistic such as:

"I am going to lose 15lbs by going to the gym three times a week, cut out carbs and by doing this I will get fitter. Because I will feel better about myself.

I may put myself on a dating website or go out to meet people twice a week and that way I have a chance of meeting a future partner and I will have written the first 2 chapters of what is going to be my bestselling novel which will make me millions".

Well that is now more definitive, measurable and achievable.

Keep your goals and targets clear and NOT fluffy.

Fluffy goals

- I am going to write a book
- I am going to lose some weight.

Good measurable goals

- I will have written the first two chapters of my best-selling novel by the end of this month
- I am going to lose 15lbs by going to the gym 3 times a week and cutting out carbs, starting on Tuesday this week.

> Being miserable is a habit;
> being happy is a habit;
> and the choice is yours.
> (Tom Hopkins)

11. Being S.M.A.R.T. about your goals

As simple formula for setting your goals by changing your habits is to use the simple and widely used SMART criteria.

SMART is an acronym, giving a short list criterion to provide a guide in helping you choosing, listing and setting your goals and objectives.

S - Simple or Specific.

Don't over complicate what you are trying to achieve and be as specific as possible, which helps make it...

M - Measurable.

"I will lose 14lbs at the rate of 2lbs a week for 7 weeks" is measurable

A - Achievable.

"I will begin a project that will make me millions" may be achievable, However, "I will make millions in 56 day's" probably isn't

R - Realistic,

If you set your goals too high and you don't achieve them, you set yourself up to fail. Often it is better to achieve your goals step by step and taste success rather than try and do so in one single bound.

T - Timely or Time related.

Make this is the right time for you to achieve your goals and change your habits. Decide what you are going to do, when you are going to do it, by when - and then DO it.

However, if you prefer to continuously improve, we would recommend you take it to the next level though and be SMARTER about your goals and objectives. How? Just add in the E and R....

E - Evaluate.

> This is why we have those exercises at the beginning and end of each week.

R - Review or Reflect.

> It is so important to reflect on what you have done, how you have done it and how you can do it better next time.

> You cannot change your future
> You cannot change your future.
> But you can change your habits.
> And surely your habits will change your future
> (Abdul Kalam)

12. The Habit Triangle

The Habit Triangle is a really simple way to look at and recognise your habitual behaviour and its impacts on you and those around you. It shows the simple process of how habitual behaviours, the kind that we just don't even think about, keep us in the same rut and give us the same often negative outcomes and the result is inevitable and you get nowhere.

Working with our own habits and behaviours and using the habit triangle it is very easy to see what we do and what we have to do to change the outcome.

By using the strength and simplicity of the habit triangle to help us change a negative habit and behaviours that go with it into positive ones we also learn to manipulate our outcomes and our future. How good is that?

The Habit triangle is an essential component and tool in the battle to change your habits. It will show you how you take the strength of a negative habit and replace it with a positive one.

In the habit triangle there are, not surprisingly, three aspects or corners to a habit or behaviour:

1. The Cue or Trigger
2. The Behaviour
3. The Result or Reward

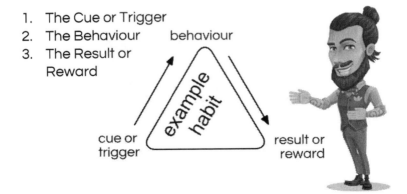

The first is the Cue or Trigger

This is the emotion, feeling, sensation, thought, in fact anything that is the initial indicator at the start of a habit.

When the process begins our instinct or habit takes over which is why we have to be aware of not only what our cue or trigger is but when we begin to realise that it has been activated.

The recognition therefore is essential to the whole process of change.

It is in the recognition of what kick starts your behaviour or negative habit and you will find some pretty strong clues as to what our Primary habit is and potentially what you Feeder habits are that support it.

The behaviour or the second part of the triangle is the direct response to your trigger. For example, if your partner talks to you in a certain tone that instantly gets your back up or in a way that you know they want something then you will automatically make assumptions and react in the same old way.

Your partners way of saying something can cause you to react in a very specific way.

Your Partners tone of voice is the trigger, you're getting riled is your habitual behaviour.

This is the part that we can work on to change, the reactive behaviour from a repeated trigger. Change that and you can change anything.

The reward or the third part of the triangle is what we gain from our behaviour. That may seem like an odd thing to say but even if the habit is negative there is always a reward for your brain. Incidentally when we talk about a reward the brain doesn't care or acknowledge if your habits and behaviours are good or bad for you, otherwise how would you explain addiction?

Using the same example of your partners voice really getting your back up, you may wonder what possible reward is there for you? Again, let me gently remind you that this is all about your brain looking for the easiest answer and that's repetition.

So, the reward for the brain in this case is just making no effort to change, it doesn't care if you end up in a row with your partner, in fact your brain prefers it if you do because it is always what you do. Habit!

The result is always either the negative or positive consequence of your behaviour or habit. By breaking the process down to three simple component parts we can begin to see the power of the triangle and the potential power of changing it for completely different rewards and results.

Of course, we haven't mentioned results yet, so let us do that now.

The result in this case is a very predictable argument set off by a seemingly simple process of a certain tone of voice and it is the result that we need to change.

Looking at this process we can simply clarify what happens in this habit triangle and it will happen in a split second.

First stage is your partners tone of voice, this has an instant impact on you and you react to it and finally the row ensues.

All of this because your partner spoke in a specific tone of voice?

No - all this including the argument is nothing to do with your partners tone, it is ALL to do with your response to the voice. You cannot control your partners voice, however irritating or ingratiating it may be, but you can always control how you respond to it.

Change that and you get complete control of what happens next and your partner will wonder what on earth is going on!

This is an example of how a negative habit can impact on your health and how changing it can have a profound impact.

A man has worked in the same factory for twenty years, he does the same job now as he did the day he started.

In the next two pages we will look at what happens in this scenario, how he reacts and behaves, what triggers that, his reward and the results.

The Trigger….

Halfway through his morning shift he checks the clock because after 20 years of doing the same job he always gets bored, very bored.

His cue or trigger is the time and the boredom. It has now become such a habit that he actually looks forward to being bored and there is a good reason for that. Every time he gets bored he rewards himself. That's right, now he is bored, he gives himself a present.

The neural pathway that we spoke of before now looks forward to and expects to be bored because the body and brain will be rewarded. But how?

That's all down to his Behaviour!

His repetitive behaviour is what he does or reverts to every time and in his own head his habit is waiting for his boredom.

As soon as the trigger happens the brain waits for the expected behaviour, in fact it has been preparing him all along.

The brain begins to send messages to his stomach in anticipation of the food he is about to get as well as the pathway for his expected reward of nicotine - the man stops his work, goes outside for a cigarette and eats a bacon sandwich.

The brain is satisfied, as is his stomach and his neurological longing for a cigarette.

The Reward...

His reward is that he is less bored, his stomach is now full, and his tobacco addiction has been fulfilled all because he is bored. However, he also now believes that he needs that break and routine in order to get through until lunchtime. In fact, if he thought that it might change then he would probably panic, but now he continues to work until lunch time, content.

The reward is clear.

The Result...

We know that eating fatty food everyday as well as smoking will probably have a huge effect on his health and despite him know that he will continue because his justification to himself is that he deserves the treat as he has such a boring job. His brain will certainly not argue because it just loves habit and doesn't care about the consequences.

However, by changing his negative behaviour to something positive, i.e. a walk around the factory and some fruit instead, his reward will be the same - he relieves his boredom, but the result will be that he loses weight, becomes healthier.

Simple to say but a massive change of habit would be required and eventually the brain would fight for the new and positive habit and not the old negative one. As the man in the factory edged towards his morning break the brain would begin to long for the freshness of the fruit and the man's legs would be looking forward to the light exercise.

Let's look at another example - Fear

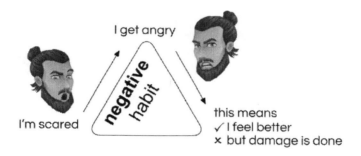

In this example, we have used fear as the trigger or cue.

Changing habits is not about changing things beyond your control but changing how we respond to them.

This is the huge premise that will give you back control of all you do despite anyone or anything happening that you have to respond to.

In this example, the reason for his fear maybe that he is frustrated and scared because of his job or relationship isn't secure for most of us this can be a pretty terrifying situation to deal with and in addition he may feel helpless to change anything, it is not possible or practical to be able to change that circumstance in the short term. But he can change how he responds to it.

The trigger therefore will remain the same because to change that would have to mean changing the circumstances that cause it and that may not be in his control.

The reward, or at least a part of it should also remain the same, i.e. in this case, his anger and frustration should and must be vented, then he feels better.

In our example the reward of his habit and behaviour was the release of anger and frustration.

The result however also included losing his temper and taking it out on someone else. The damaging and sometimes irreversible impact of extreme anger and sometimes violence can change many lives, permanently.

Again, then the intervening habit or behaviour is key to our control of the situation and the outcome of it.

Returning to our example, rather than directing anger at someone or something he looked to take that pent-up energy and turn it to a "double positive" result, for example going for a run or lifting some weights or walking. In fact, anything not to immediately "lose it"

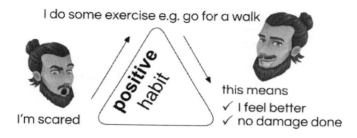

Often in cases where there is anger involved it can take a long time to reverse a deeply rooted habit, but even though this is a clear and frightening example there is no reason why this habit is any more deep-set than any other.

Acceptance of change and knowing how to change, and by keeping the trigger and reward the same, the brain has far less to learn and the habit becomes positive!

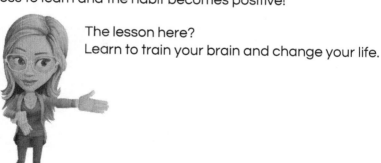

The lesson here?
Learn to train your brain and change your life.

13. Intellect and not emotion

One of our favourite sayings about habits is:

'Your beliefs become your thoughts, your thoughts become your words, your words become your actions, your actions become your habits, your habits become your values and your values become your destiny'

It is right to say that the process of using the habit changing handbooks is relying on your intellect and not your emotion as we are re training our brains to think and react in a very different way. That is not to say that emotion does not have a part to play, it does. The part that emotion plays is being aware of how you are feeling, it's more of a warning system so that the intellect can take over and steer the brain to make the correct decision and not just react as it would have done so before.

As the saying at the top of the page says this is about changing control from the beginning of your subconscious thoughts.

It starts with belief

Imagine for a moment that you could see all of your core, solid, non-shakeable beliefs all lined up together?

- How would they look?
- Would you recognize them?
- Understand how they got to be that way in the first place?
- Would you happily share them with everyone that knows you?
- Maybe, maybe not?

The thing with beliefs is that we often inherit them from our parents, family, friends and surrounding influences such as school, religion or television and social media. How do we know that they are ours? Have you ever checked? These are after all the very foundations of who you are.

Now look at the next step of the saying, "Your beliefs become Your thoughts."

YOUR thoughts?

Your thoughts may not even belong to you, they may have been inherited from a bygone era, you may have been force fed them and yet we all accept them as ours. But why?

Following on from that logic, we are what we believe, therefore so that we use intellect to check on our beliefs let's keep emotion out of it, because unless we change our beliefs how can we change our thoughts and therefore ourselves.

Of course, the other possibility is that you don't actually have any particularly strong beliefs on anything.

Maybe you consider yourself open minded and liberal. Non-judgemental and fluid of thought. That's Ok but then sometimes it may give you an issue around formatting clear thoughts and actions and getting stuff done or focusing could be a problem

If you want to, if you dare, write down what you believe are your main beliefs about you and your attitude to life in general but especially yourself...Go on I dare you

How was that? I hope you took your time and was honest with yourself, it's all about learning!

With all of that said it is hugely important that we remember that this is about intellect!

Some of us of course do tend to rely on instinct and we are often reminded that we should listen to the little voice sharing its wisdom from within.

That's terrific, why not?

All we ask is that listening to something that is from the gut, or in your waters or frankly feeling it in your fingers or your toes is one thing, following the advice/feeling is something else.

Listen, balance, think, decide - Use intellect and not emotion.

14. Belief

As already alluded to belief in something, especially in yourself, is the bedrock of thought, words, action, habit, values and destiny.

So, take it seriously!

Sometimes belief in ourselves or lack of it is the only thing that is holding us back, it's also nearly always the hardest part to achieve.

It's no wonder that many people have difficulty in believing in themselves. We have been listening to self-induced doubt brought on from parents, teachers, friends, images that are all around us and that incessant voice banging away in our heads telling us we are not good enough!!

Recognise that? Do you have a voice?

How would you like to shut that voice up once and for all? How would you like a positive voice that completely believes in you without any doubts? A voice that encourages and promotes, knows you, trusts you and your judgement, totally? Imagine the difference to the things that you could do, the life choices and changes you make?

You can, right now. Self-belief is just a state of mind, an intellectual decision, your decision.

From the beginning of this book it is essential that at some level you believe enough in yourself and your ability to achieve. Believing that you can do this, change your habits and change your life is probably the hardest part your journey. Sometimes even the strongest of faiths can be tested when the pressure is on. However, belief or lack of it is also habit and it can be changed.

But what is belief?

'Belief is a state of mind in which a person thinks something to be the case without there being any evidence to prove that this is the case with factual certainty'.

Many organisations make great importance of having a faith and belief in a higher power and many reformed addicts swear that only by giving into a power greater than themselves are they able to remain clear of their addiction.

This has proved to be very successful for many thousands of people but not all and why is that?

It has proven to be a little bit more complicated than simple acceptance and belief in a higher entity.

After many psychological studies it appears that it is not having faith in a higher power or God, it is not a belief in something specific, it is about belief itself.

But frankly what the heck does that even mean?

Well look back at the definition of the word belief. It is about belief without proof, it's not about belief in something specific and here is the subtle but discernible difference. It is the process of belief that matters.

Look at it this way, belief is the action of taking a step without knowing where you are going, it is about trust. The definition of trust is: belief in the integrity, ability, or character of a person or thing; confidence or reliance:

So, is that it? The belief and trust in your own ability for change, your own integrity and having confidence and reliance in you.

You are asking then for a leap of faith and that triggers the brain to be open and ready to be informed and to change. That is the process that belief and faith give us, an open portal for change.

So, to make the most of this book and gain all that you want to from it will require total self-belief? Well, yes and no.

In the process of working out your Primary Habit and then replacing one Feeder Habit with one Builder Habit every week, you are creating more self-belief because you are seeing the changes in yourself.

It is a fundamental part of change and by following the simple steps in this book you can build self-belief, learn to trust your own judgement, change your habits, hit your goal and change your life.

The structure of how the book works is to allow your belief to grow, step by step.

With each feeder habit conquered and each builder habit put in place your belief in yourself grows.

Setting and aiming for habit changes every week feeds your growth, self-expectation and self-belief.

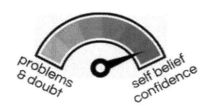

15. Breathing & Focusing

Most of us if we are lucky take the fact that we breathe easily for granted. Many however, those suffering from some kind of breathing or lung disorders, do not.

Why is this relevant to changing Habits? It is a great tool for control.

One thing is for certain, at some stage of our lives if not every stage most of us take the miracle that is breathing for granted.

Not only does our body do it without us thinking about how or when we breathe, it just gets on with it.

What we rarely appreciate is what a powerful indicator of our state of mind our breathing is

If we are anxious or nervous our breathing increases and is shallow, if we are relaxed and at peace our breathing is deeper and slower. So, to be more relaxed and more at peace we should always breathe more slowly?

Why not?

Controlling our breathing through simple mindfulness exercises helps control anxiety and aides focusing and concentration on the here and now. This in turn creates an escape, a place to be at peace with yourself and all that is around you.

During your journey through the hand book, focusing on why you are breaking negative habits and creating positive ones will require some calm contemplation.

Controlled breathing and mindfulness are a psychologically proven way to better our health both mental and physical.

Try if you will for a couple of minutes be aware of your breathing, its effects on your body and how deep or shallow your breaths are. Once you can feel and are in touch with your natural breathing rhythm consciously change it and note how different you feel.

Conscious breathing will also help you to respond more positively and make the right choices for your day.

Making choices about our day is something, a bit like breathing that we do without thinking and a little like the way we breath, it makes a huge difference to the quality of our moment, our day and our lives.

Replace these with Beliefs.

Moral excellence comes about as a result of habit. We become just by doing just acts, temperate by doing temperate acts, brave by doing brave acts
(Aristotle)

16. Gratitude

One of the greatest if not the greatest under- utilized mindsets has to be gratitude

When it comes to changing habits and changing lives we need to understand the Why as we have already discussed in the section on goals.

However, looking at what we have, appreciating the good things in life however simple can give us a solid basis on which to build and grow.

Without gratitude for what we have now how can we ever appreciate what we are hoping to build and create. What marker do we have to measure by, how quickly would we take it all for granted and then find ourselves back where we started.

It may seem counter intuitive to be grateful for a life that you are desperate to change but without it your changing will amount to nothing but a blip, a short term positive before you slip back into negativity.

The habit of Gratitude is a Habit that will serve you well for all of your life, it brings perspective and clarity, peace and wellbeing and a stage on which to build.

Rather than write down and re-read the things that you are grateful for every day, recent psychological observations and thinking is that this is an exercise that should be done once a week.

The Habit Changing Handbook

After every seven days when you complete a week's feeder and builder habit change, write down everything, including what you have been grateful for in the last week, and everything that you have achieved. That will bring into focus just how well you are doing and is a strong reflection of your success in habit changing and this helps you in your growing self-belief.

Try not to write the same things every time as the more you look beyond your normal circle of gratitude the more you will see positivity in all things around you.

This exercise will increase the positive energy around you and with your weekly achievements written down and confirmed to you, your belief in yourself and what you are doing will grow.

Of course, be grateful for your loved ones and your health perhaps or the fact you live in a vibrant area or somewhere tranquil if you prefer but start to look beyond that to smaller normally over-seen things.

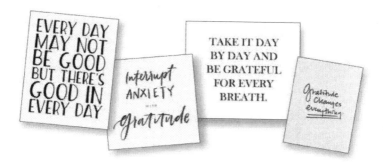

Here is a list of some suggestions but please find plenty for yourself:

- A good night's rest
- The colour of the trees in the changing seasons
- A warm or cool breeze
- The lessons we learn from our children
- Knowing you are OK today
- Hot showers

A few things that you should know about writing gratitude lists. These are some results you should expect if you do this every day or weekly but always consistently...

- It's tough at first
- There is always something to be grateful for
- It's rarely about material things
- Gratitude grows the more you use it
- You become more positive
- It helps stop negative thought patterns
- You develop a belief that the world is fundamentally good
- Life becomes more enjoyable

Lastly, this is an important part of your habit changing handbook journey and with the attitude towards positive habits becoming more ingrained with scientific understanding this is a way to feel very different very quickly and it all fast tracks you to changing those negative habits.

Gratitude is totally empowering to you and those around you, embrace the habit and you will feel the difference immediately.

17. Choosing to win or lose

Would it surprise you to know that every day we choose whether to have a good day or have a bad day?

It is another habit that we do without thinking and it impacts on absolutely everything that we do, experience and live with.

Win or Lose
Its _your_ choice

Choosing to win or lose is a daily decision that we all make - what did you decide this morning?

Did you wake up and think to yourself that whatever the day throws at you, whatever your boss says, however much rain falls on you even though it is the worst day of the week for you, that you were going to have a good day and make it a day that counts, one where you choose to win despite everything?

Or, maybe the very thought of all of that did your head struggle off the pillow and did you feel in the pit of your stomach the dread of a bad day ahead and choosing to lose the day just seemed like the only option?

It's not - Those decisions are based on habit.

If you choose to have a bad day then surely enough you will have one because your brain is expecting it, you are attracting it and all you will see is a grotty day that just can't end soon enough.

What a waste!

On the other hand, deciding to have a good day, whatever happens the very least you have is a positive attitude even if the day isn't great you are one step ahead. You will also be looking for the positive, attracting the positive and only choosing to see the positive.

A day gained - a day won.

Why don't you make a decision and start from now?

1. Make the decision - choose to have a good day.

2. Hold onto that thought and that feeling.

3. See how it changes the results of your day.

Your day - Your decision!

Often, we will know someone that can seem irritatingly positive even in the worst of circumstances. Somehow, they seem happy in the face of all adversity but mainly just in a better place than most of us.

Does it mean that they have secretly won the lottery?
- Maybe but probably not.

Perhaps they walk around in their own micro climate?
- I don't think so

Or...

maybe they have a secret to their positivity and happiness?
- Probably, and now so do you.

I'm not suggesting this is going to be easy, in fact it's a major change for most of us. There will inevitably be many mornings when however much you try your brain just won't let go of bad habits and you are in for a rough day.

The solution to this like so much when it comes to Habits is recognizing what is happening to you, see how that decision has impacted on your day. Hopefully this will give you more resolve to push that little bit harder the next morning. Be aware of good and bad, positive and negative. Start to search for change.

Habit is only repeated behaviours so start to repeat the good ones... you will change.

Choosing to see only positivity in your life will, like any habit, soon become subconscious and even when things do go wrong, this is life after all, your brain will instinctively look for the positive. It will have trained itself to react to a bad situation, through habit

Why would you ever choose to have a bad day again?

It's your decision!

18. Thinking and Communication

The Habit Changer Hand series are designed to change the way that you think, that in turn will change the way that you respond and then the way that you feel.

Your twenty-eight-day habit changing exercise is designed specifically to re train your brain by showing you how to change age old habits that have become so ingrained that the habits themselves control your life how you perceive life and how life sees you.

Taking back control and DECIDING to change behaviours to your advantage will transform your outlook, your possibilities and your freedoms throughout your life.

A wonderful man by the name of Viktor Frenkl wrote in a compelling book "Man's search for meaning" the following:

"Everything can be taken from a man but one thing, the last of human freedoms-to choose one's attitude in any given set of circumstances, to choose one's own way... Between stimulus and response there is a space. In that space is our power to choose our response. In our response lies our growth and freedom"

What he was getting at is that we have a choice in how we respond to people and circumstances even though we may have been pre- programmed by upbringing, circumstance and our own habits to respond in certain ways, we can change all of that and change our lives.

Referring back to the Habit Triangle you can change the word 'cue' to the word 'stimulus' and 'behaviour' to 'response' and what is being reinforced is the link between how we respond in our behaviour to the changing results that we will see.

The one thing for certain is that using Frenkl's mixture of philosophical and psychological referencing, we require a small amount of effort to change, for a life time's reward.

Shortly after 'Man's search for meaning 'was first published, Eric Berne a renowned Psychiatrist, started to work on a therapeutic theory called 'Transactional Analysis'

One of the founding bed rocks of this work, that still thrives today is the well-known therapeutic model called PAC. It is this model, which again emphasizes that we respond in particular ways, responding out of habit.

However, in this section we can begin to see how, by responding reactively we create a response from others who are equally 'reacting'. What I mean by that, is that all of our relationships be they personal or work, loved ones, family or friends rely on and are created by the way that we communicate.

This is undoubtedly the most over looked habit of all. Control of it changes everything. By changing how we respond to other people we can also change the response of others to us and change relationships and negative habits.

In simplistic terms the PAC stands for: Parent, Adult or Child

We need to remember that it's not just how we react to what people say, but also how THEY say it.

Did you know that when we are talking with someone this is how the brain works out what is going on?

- only 7% of meaning is in the words spoken,
- 38% is from the way in which the words are said, and
- 55% is in the facial expression being used!

It explains how we often get the wrong message and, in a time when much of our communication is by words alone, i.e. texting we can begin to see how difficult it is to know exactly what is being said and why so many misunderstandings occur.

We all tend to respond from the point of view of one of these ego states most of the time and I am sure that you will recognise perhaps your own position and potentially those of others around you by looking at the diagram here.

The 'Parent' State.

The Parent state can be either a Critical parent or a Nurturing parent.

A critical parent may be seen as someone who insists on rules, lots of 'shoulds' and 'musts'. Real expectations of themselves and those around them.

- Think of a "finger wagging nag"

Perhaps your own biological parents were like this or one was, maybe a teacher or other important adult in your life as a child or even now.

Can you think of someone that surrounds themselves with rules and can't see how they or others can function without them?

Maybe that's you?

The Habit Changing Handbook

A nurturing parent can mean unconditional loving, optimistic and over-hopeful ego state.

In theory this sounds perfect but sometimes this could potentially lead to no real boundaries around these people and consequently some people find it hard to pin them down or they may dither or procrastinate rather than make a decision or have a conversation that may potentially upset someone.

These people may spoil their children and certainly they would never see the bad in them, sadly there is a bit of bad in all of us.

Both of the above have positive and negative aspects. For example, rules tend to be what keeps a civilisation together, think laws etc. but the extreme is a dictatorship. The nurturing parent can be blindly optimistic and sometimes doesn't see or want to see what is in front of them.

The 'Adult' state.

The adult is where, in this habit changing process, we should aim to be. It is a part of yourself that is logical, rational and clear thinking. It can analyse what is happening and act accordingly.

It is neither bossy nor dominated but listens and makes a decision.

This ego state is reliable and does not knee jerk but rather balances the options and makes an 'adult' decision

Of course, nobody is perfect but like all habits when it comes to communication this is something that can be practiced and learnt.

Perhaps this is where you see yourself? What would others say?

The 'Child' state

This can be either an 'Adaptive' or a 'Free' child.

The Adaptive child stems from the emotional, the biological and the environmental circumstances they find themselves in.
- This is what we are going to avoid.

Quite often with the child ego states the person has been or is being dominated by someone who spends much of their time in Parent mode. It can be fairly obvious in body language, the two feet sometimes at an angle pointing towards each other, the tone of voice even the way that some people dress might suggest being trapped in a child ego state.

The Free child is spontaneous and creative and lives in the moment but rarely plans or is interested in changes. Again, we should not be here.

Both of the child states can also be useful places to be at different times. The Adaptive child can pull on experience of the past and the Free child is the perfect place to be when you need to have fun, be in the moment.

The upshot of this is that when communicating with each other, be that work colleagues or with friends or family, we see, hear and respond in that ego state. It also means that we react to someone else that is in their own.

The Habit Changing Handbook

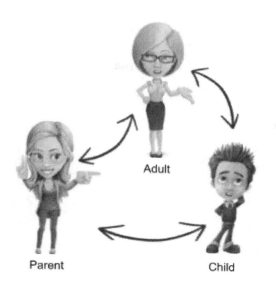

We should point out here that although we are depicting the child state with a child character we actually mean a person acting in a child state.

And while we're at it, we know that men can be adults and parents too!

And before you say anything – men can be children too!

Let's look at these relationships with an example

"If I see the world and communicate with all the time form the point of Parent and my best friend is always stuck in child, our relationship will always fall back to that and be highly restrained because of it.

Perhaps my friend the child hates being spoken to by me in that parental way but because they are in a child ego state they would never say.

They may however resent it or even sulk. If we both become trapped in our behaviour we could both be pretty unhappy in our friendship but neither of us can let go, I won't because at some fundamental level feel that they, my friend could not cope without me and anyhow I can't let them down and they won't stop because of the same reason plus they would feel a bit lost".

The result - both are trapped.

If they could find a way to communicate differently they would either find a far better relationship or actually decide they don't like each other? It's a risk but it's real.

Do you recognise yourself in any of these descriptions?

None of us have to stay in these ego states and in truth we should always be able to move between them for when it is appropriate. After all, in a time of emergency it's probably always better to be in either Adult or even Parent, taking control in a chaotic situation can require a strong wagging finger.

On the other hand, there are times when being in child mode is ideal and very appropriate but being able to choose and being able to recognize where you and others are is hugely powerful.

'We are what we repeatedly do.
Excellence, then, is not an act, but a habit
(Aristotle)

The Habit Changing Handbook

19. The Parent Adult Child Model (PAC)

Below are a couple of situations you may find yourself in and then three simple responses. Consider these and see if you can identify from what position as a parent adult or child, you would respond from.

Scenario 1.

A member of your team or work colleague asks you for some information that is clearly and easily available if they make the effort. How do you reply?

"Hi, yes of course I will find it for you, no problem. How are you? Is there anything else I can do for you?"

"Don't be so lazy, look for yourself"

"Have a look around and see if you can find it, if you have a problem get back to me but it's good for you to find your way around and get comfortable with the format"

Scenario 2.

You have started your habit journal and one of your feeder habits is eating more healthily. On the third day of changing this habit you have a bad day and you walk past a shop that sells your favourite chocolate. Three responses are:

"To hell with it I've done really well I deserve it, it's only a couple of bars"

"God how weak am I? I'm really rubbish at this I'm so weak"

"I'm doing really well and as much as I want one I'll be strong for one more day, this will pass."

Write down which one related to P, A or C and see if you recognise how you would normally react.

These are all habits, and with work you can change them.

The reason that this is so important when it comes to changing habits is simply because these are not just conversations and relationships with friends and family, it's also what goes on in your own head.

This really refers back to taking a moment to think, changing your behaviour to change the outcome taking back control and not accepting negativity.

These conversations in our own head between parent and child feeling guilty and then not caring can be very destructive.

Again, this is just another tool for you to listen and watch what you do to others and to yourself.

Communication in this context is about the words, to yourself and to others. If it comes from belief and your belief is the best it can be, so will your words and communication to yourself and others.

Often in relationships both at home and at work we can see and feel the habitual way in which we respond to each other. This habitual communication often gets us stuck in a routine that can be damaging to our relationship.

As an example, you may have a partner or relation who, according to you always speaks in a certain way especially when they want something. That tone of voice somehow has an immediate impact on you and you respond to that voice in the same way.

Look at the situation below.

The voice in this example is whiney and child-like and you find yourself chastising this person for whining and instantly reacting from the position of Parent.

By doing this of course your partner sticks in 'Child'.

After your rebuke the expected exchange from BOTH of your viewpoints is inevitable and destructive. It is a repeated behaviour that always ends badly.

So, what can you do? How can you change it and frankly, what difference will it make if they just keep whining?

By changing your 'automatic' habitual response. I.e. not responding when your back gets up and becoming all Parent. That is what you can do. You can take control of and change what happens now.

The difference it will make is that by you refusing to react from Parent and always reacting from Adult, eventually so will your partner. It is almost impossible to keep stuck where you are on the PAC model if the other person moves their position.

Let's see how that works, firstly let's look at the fixed behaviour and communication before any changes.

For this example, Hardy will be the whiner and Alice will be the impatient partner.

Hardy enters the room yawning.

"I'm really tired, I've been working all day. I know I said that I would get the tiling done tonight, but I just don't have the time, I have so much to do!"

Alice immediately feels the hairs in the back of her neck rise as soon as she hears the first 'I'm really tired' She notes in a micro second that his shoulders are slumped, his feet are facing inward, and his bottom lip is almost quivering. He is also making his way towards the stairs and his office.

Alice's shoulders go back and as she feels the anger rise from her stomach she immediately responds:

"I've been waiting months for this and the house is a total wreck. It's just a pathetic excuse. Why can't you get yourself organised? You always find time for other stuff!"

Hardy, having received the opening salvo from Alice, retreats further into Child.

"Well I didn't want to do it in the first place and I said that I would get it done as soon as I had a chance and I DON'T STOP, YOU KNOW THAT! and if you want it done so badly why don't you do it yourself! Oh no I forgot, you can't!

I'll do it as soon as I can."

Alice, now standing over him and wagging her finger. 'You make me so mad with all of your promises - You are such a disappointment you are going to finish it tonight whether you like it or not and that's the end of it!'

The Habit Changing Handbook

That went well!

Clearly this is a relationship that could do with a bit of a change. So, let's replay the same conversation with Alice changing the dynamics.

Hardy entered the room...

"I'm really tired, I've been working all day. I know I said that I would get the tiling done tonight, but I just don't have the time, I have so much to do!"

Alice has decided to act in Adult/Parent to Hardy's clear Child Ego state. She replies:

'I know how busy you are and I'm really sorry to keep going on but it would mean so much to me if we could just get this finished. How can I help, perhaps if I can help you with your work then you could make time to finish the job? I really understand the pressure that you are under

'What would you like to eat before we go up?"

Ok I have been putting it off, haven't I? Any chance of a quick toastie?

Ok, this was a bit simplified, but the message is clear. By changing her reaction Alice got a far more positive response as there was very little for Hardy to push against. He really had to move towards adult, if not completely embracing it.

If you remain in Adult, whatever is thrown at you by any other party and from whatever ego state it comes from it will eventually have to shift to Adult, always.

The dynamics changed for this one conversation but imagine all you could do? - All you could change?

Perhaps there has always been a person in your life that you have always had a difficult relationship with? A parent, spouse, sibling, friend, boss or colleague. Change your habits in the way you respond to them and change your relationship forever.

There are many relationships that have built in 'habitual rituals. These are often in families but also at work and with friends.

These interactions are ALL built on how we react to one another. Its ALL about habit.

The Habit Changing Handbook gives you choice and control. However, we all face one more 'nay-sayer' more powerful than the rest.

I was once at a wedding where during the best man's speech, he was a murder detective by the way but funny anyway, told us all in the audience to do something rather romantic. He said, 'I want you all to take a moment and if they are here with you on this joyous day, look deeply into the eyes of your life partner'.

All of us a little self-consciously did just that and amongst some giggles the whole room of nearly 300 people were looking deeply into the eyes of their loved ones.

The best man took a moment and then said with no tone of irony 'you are all looking into the eyes of the person who is the most likely person on this earth... to murder you! '

He enjoyed the gasps and laughs and then gave us some statistics from his job to prove his point.

Q: Why would I repeat this story?
A: It is highly relevant.

The person most likely to stop you achieving what you want in life, to metaphorically stab you in the back is the one closest to you and one you would never suspect.

With all of those people that have told you forever that you are not good enough, all of those finger nagging nags, those negative whisperers none of these will stop you.

However, look deeply into the eyes of the person who stares back at you in the mirror and there…. There, in the mirror is the culprit, the destroyer of your dreams.

No one else - Just you.

Often the conversations around PAC can be played out in our heads and not just with a third party.

These are the conversations that you can begin to change, and you can begin right now.

Do not listen to the voice that says, 'yes I know I will get on with it later' or the one that says, 'it's alright for others but not for me?'

Instead, recognize the voices in your own head respond in Adult and begin to control your destiny.

20. A letter to your future self

The thought of this may seem at the very least, a little bit odd. However, it is not only proven through loads of psychological papers that it works, it's a statement.

Writing to yourself is an expression of where you are now a snap shot in time. The process is already connecting with the future you and reaffirming the direction and goals that you want for yourself. It can also be an expression of hope and desire, a forecasting of where you want to be from where you are now. A confirmation of intent, a voice that you must listen to. Your voice.

The letter should not be a liturgy of apologies or excuses but rather be an optimistic and hopeful expression of where you are going to be.

Look forward not backward.

The Habit Changing Handbook

It should have energy and substance, when you read this back to yourself in twenty-eight days' time you will hear a voice from your past and you will be fulfilling the dreams of the person you left behind.

The letter should also be personal and in your own style. There is an example letter online at www.habitchanger.co.uk/letter

Be very careful and exact about how you are expecting to feel, choose to be positive and choose to win. Do not expect or tolerate failure in any way, cheer yourself on to the winning post and visualise the different, in control you.

When you write the letter put it in an envelope and post it to yourself. Don't just write it and put it away - put a stamp on it and actually put it in the post box! Posting the letter to yourself is psychologically a very important step. You are sending the letter to the future you, a different you. Do this the day you start the, don't star to change your habits. Don't start anything until you have done this.

When you letter arrives place it somewhere safe.

Some people prefer to hide it somewhere out of sight, others prefer to keep it close at hand, to be constantly reminded of its presence and significance.

It will be a source of anticipation and of determination as you travel through your journey establishing a sense of purpose, success and of self and all for the person that wrote the letter to you on who's hopes for the future are riding on you.

21. Putting it all together.

It's pretty safe to say that we all have habits. Your habits are part of what makes you who you are, your personality, your character. You go through life with your collection of habits, some are good, others are not-so-good, some are bad, and some are destructive if not dangerous!

So, it could be fair to say that you can change your life by managing if not changing those very habits - capitalising on the good ones and replacing the bad negative habits with other, more positive, helpful habits instead.

The actual word "habit" has different meanings, but in our context, we use the word to describe any pattern of behaviour you carry out time and time again with little thought or effort, usually automatically, and without thinking.

The habit changing handbooks, a combination of self-assessment, setting goals, and journaling is a very effective way of helping you build on your good habits, and overcome those bad habits that interfere with your life.

It is so effective that even addictions are effectively treated by changing the underlying habits that contribute to them.

Just take a simple example of a smoker who habitually lights up when he or she is on the phone, leaves the building, gets in the car or has a coffee. Their body may be addicted to the nicotine but it's the supporting feeder habits that are fuelling and maintaining that addiction.

You don't need to be a rocket scientist to work out that by changing the feeder habit the addiction opportunity for the indulgence of the addiction is lessened.

The Habit Changing Handbook

Reflections and journaling are two other very useful tools in your armoury in getting you to who and where you want to be.

Reflections

Take a moment each day to lookback of what you have achieved and appreciate all you have done, or not done to get closer to the goal that you know will change your life. You could do this simply by asking yourself three simple questions before you end the day

1. How well did I do what I did today?
2. What have I learned from this?
3. What can I do tomorrow better?

It's an important moment in the day so try to set a specific time to reflect, perhaps when first in bed.

Journaling

It would help immensely if you could write down your reflections and your thoughts and feelings regarding your journey on a daily basis.

This process of journaling has been proven time and time again to have a reinforcing power second to none.

When you get to the end of the first week and you have replaced your negative feeder habit for your constructive builder habit, make sure you write down what you have achieved and reward yourself. Never belittle your daily, weekly and life time achievement. It can be tough so appreciate all you do and write it down.

22. Summary

The Habit Changer Handbook to stop Procrastination is a book to keep close at hand. We have looked at what habits are and why we have them and how they can impact o so much of your life. All of that is of no use unless you have a way, if you want to, to change or create habits.

The mechanism that is described in some detail in the book, Primary, Feeder and Builder habits is a structured way to change, but of course you do actually have to do it.

The book also looks at where we so often go wrong when it comes to making changes. The simple process of looking at why we want to change and what we will gain in our lives and how will it change us? Without the knowledge of where we are going and what we want change for then it is a waste of time and doomed to failure.

We have also looked at the huge importance of Belief and how the lack of it stops us achieving all that we want. The book shows a way to build your self- belief through small but important changes.

Belief of course is just one part of the mindset for change, the use of breath control and gratitude all help to lay the pathway for change. With no foundations, however wonderful the new structure of habits and behaviour is, it will fall. Make your foundations strong and you can build yourself a new life, getting things done and beating, at last, Procrastination.

This book has set out to empower you, to create new habits, and replace those old ones that have kept you subconsciously trapped in negative behaviours.

And now you have the toolkit to change.

In this book you now have a framework for you to change the habits that have been holding you back. By following this therapeutically based process, converting them into habits that will support your development and growth into the person that you want to be.

This book is an easy to use friendly companion, not a text book or checklist. Instead it is set out as a simple and straight-forward daily routine which creates an expectation of completion and success.

The strong belief that will manifest itself over the coming weeks will enable you to conquer your previous limited self-expectation whilst creating a structured template for you to plan, organise and achieve any goal you set yourself.

The Habit Changing Handbook will "open the door to your future" all you have to do is walk through.

We're only human, so, during this journey you shouldn't expect perfection, rather you should embrace the challenges, learn from your mistakes and celebrate your victories.

So, without any further ado,
let's get going.

Enjoy, and have fun!

Cheerio!

23. Stories

These stories are real cases of what has been achieved by changing habits.

The names have been changed but in every other way each case is a genuine real-life story.

The purpose of sharing these real-life stories is to maybe trigger some thoughts of your own, and better understand how other people have used this simple process to change and/or improve themselves by controlling and improving their habits.

The Habit Changing Handbook

Diana's story

When Diana first came across the Habit Changer it took her nearly three months to actually find time to read it. She kept meaning to, it was just that so many other things kept getting priority. In fact, pretty much everything got in the way of Diana's quest for change. You see Diana's problem was her total devotion to the act of procrastination.

Diana is a mum of three and a wife to Derek. She works from home and all of her children are now at school so to some degree her time is her own and this is what causes Diana her biggest headache. Her business was going nowhere, stuff wasn't getting done around the house and her husband wondered what on earth she did all day, and Diana wondered too.

Every day she would be determined to break her cycle of list after list, distraction after distraction finishing her day with disappointment and despondency.

Diana started to work with the Habit Changer and she figured pretty quickly that the feeder habits would lead her to the builder habits that she needed.

She stopped writing lists and instead made the decision to only go onto social media at 9 am for an hour and 8pm. She really struggled to do this initially and even felt anxious that she was missing out somehow with all that was going on, so she replaced this feeder habit with two short phone calls to her best friends once a day. Although the communication was there having a conversation for a restricted time only allowed her much more time.

She also understood that even though she had time she was always busy or, so it seemed and most of that was indecision.

So, her next feeder habit to recognize and stop was over thinking she replaced it with her own 5 second rule. That meant that every time she caught herself thinking about doing something, rather than delay she set herself the target of doing it or starting it in just 5 seconds. This was revolutionary. It became a game that she learnt to love and she saw her decision time and action time slashed. She was getting stuff done.

Then of course she began to feel more confident so going into the third week she changed the feeder habit of watching too much TV and she replaced it with spending time with her children.

In the last of her four weeks Diana finally changed the time she went to bed so that she was refreshed and ready to go, starting earlier and finishing stronger.

What Diana managed to do in just four weeks completely transformed her business, her home life and her relationship with her husband and children. One unexpected benefit was that she felt much calmer and the other odd thing? Her relationships with both of her friends seemed to find a new meaning and quality.

Change is never easy, and Diana still works at changing and she still keeps building her self-confidence.

Time to reflect...

- What have you taken from this story?

- Are there any similarities between Diana's story and your own tendencies to keep putting things off, to procrastinate and not get things done?

The Habit Changing Handbook

Harry's Story

Getting up in the morning was a problem for Harry.

For that matter doing anything that required physical excursion was a problem! He did however want to look and feel very different than he did at this stage in his life. He knew of course that by doing virtually nothing that his health would continue to suffer but that wasn't his biggest concern, no, his biggest problem was the way he looked.

Harry had been overweight for most of his life. He could not remember ever feeling or looking anything other than fat. He was nicknamed Big H when at school and it had stuck, and it had hurt. The problem was he lived up to his name.

Harry wanted to change. He had tried every diet but continued to go back to what he did best, eat and sit.

Harry was introduced to The Habit Changer and was initially disappointed that it only spoke of habit changing. He knew of course that he ate too much and exercised too little so was it a diet he needed? well he thought so but that had never worked before.

The biggest problem Harry had was that he was just lazy, he couldn't be bothered to do anything and if he tried it didn't last and he soon gave up and went back to his old ways.

Harry wanted change.

After reading the book Harry decided that his Primary habit was procrastination - he always put things off.

He always made plans for change, in fact lots of plans but then he couldn't quite get around to the work or discipline to even start let alone complete changes in his life.

So that was it, he needed to stop putting stuff off, to stop procrastinating.

Once Harry had made his decision to change he looked at all of the Feeder habits that kept his face in the fridge and his bum on the chair, not at the same time of course.

He recognized the small things such as how much TV he watched, so he replaced that feeder habit with the builder habit of reading at least one book a week about personal development.

When he read he ate fruit instead of crisps.

He replaced the habit of keeping beer at home with treating himself to going to the pub two nights a week with enough for just one pint in his pocket.

Not only did he drink a lot less he also started to walk, exercise and socialize.

Through these small changes Harry began to feel the difference and felt something new for him, hope.

Harry changed just small habits and his favourite new habit was the 5 second rule.

This rule was simple…

Whenever he knew he had to do something, however small, and he heard the voice in his head say, 'I'll do it later' Harry would jump up and start the process of doing that task within in 5 seconds.

Sometimes to be truthful he felt ridiculous but most of the time he felt very positive about what he was doing and soon he became excellent at the 5 second rule. It became a habit. Stuff started to happen, and new habits developed. Harry almost cried when the scales began to change.

After completing the Habit Changer Harry went to a diet club. This time he did not put off changes, this time he believed in himself because he knew he was capable of change.

Harry knows his body may not yet be the toned Adonis that he longs for, but he is immensely proud of the changes he has made and spent the summer on the beach, shirt off and feeling good.

The Habit changer changed Harry's mindset, his outlook, his body, his health and his life. All because he changed his habits.

Time to reflect...

- What have you taken from this story?
- Are there any similarities between Harry's story and your own? Not just in not managing time effectively and procrastinating, but in your particular primary habit you want to change or improve.

Appendix 1. Example Feeder Habits Chart

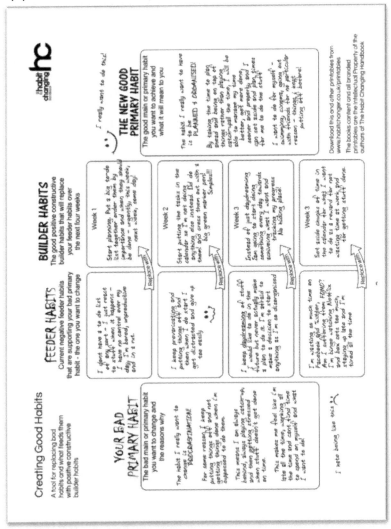

Available to read online at habitchanger.co.uk/printables

The Habit Changing Handbook

Appendix 2. Procrastination Vs Proactivation

Procrastinators – people who delay or put things off – often have the same thoughts when a new task or project lands on their lap or pops up in a reminder: "Is now a good time to finish working on that because I've only got two weeks left to do it, so that I can get started on that other project that needs to be finished the week after that?"

Then there are the obvious other blockages....

you still haven't finished what you should have started weeks ago.

and that report you have to do by tomorrow – I haven't even started that yet.

How am I supposed to cook dinner tonight for my family when I've got all this to do? Damn, I need to get to the supermarket too!

Does that sound at all familiar?

If it does, then you might also be someone that occasionally pulls a late-nighter – or even an all-nighter to finish a task that was assigned weeks ago, but you've left it to the last minute, again, before having to finish it with hours, even minutes to spare.

Do you really need that stress?

When this happens, you might blame yourself for your lack of discipline, your lack of time management maybe even your laziness, your inability to concentrate and ignore distractions. What you have here isn't any of those things – you suffer from a case of a bad procrastination habit – supported by bad time management, poor planning, not being organised, and in reality, tired and unmotivated, bowing under the pressure of an increasing pile of stuff that never seems to get done.

Remember the six P's? ...

"Proper Planning Prevents a Pathetic & Poor Performance"

And how about that oh-so-true saying:

Most people don't plan to fail they just fail to plan!

For many of us procrastinators, the answer might simply be a case of not switching on the Xbox or PlayStation or not opening that you-tube link your friend sent you, which then results in you binge watching the other videos that YouTube put in your line of sight.

For other procrastinators however, procrastination has become a habit and that can be a real problem. Procrastinating or suffering from a procrastination habit can seriously and negatively effect your life, professionally and socially, weigh down on your self-esteem, and wreck your well-being.

According to one clinical neuropsychologist, Procrastination can even be fear-related or anxiety-based. For example, if you are scared about doing badly in an exam, staff assessment or presentation, you might avoid studying and preparing for it altogether and accept the failure as "a given" and not just as just as a possibility. If you keep doing this, if you are used to doing this you might never truly do well in anything, because you won't even try.

Perfectionism, the desire or need for everything to be finished shiny and perfect is often seen as a good quality. However, that expectation by others, or even you assuming that expectation from others for you to be perfect can cause anxiety, which gets in the way and results in procrastination – putting off or dragging on as long as possible the start date of a project or of finishing what you need to do.

Clinical neuropsychologist Dr Lee said, "You become anxious, subconsciously or consciously, when you take out an assignment and you instantly find yourself relieved when you put it away," Lee says. "This is a form of internal reward."

That misplaced feeling of reward feels good, so putting off the task easily becomes a habit. This is one reason why many people fail to get things done, sometimes al all if not in time.

So, how do we stop this debilitating procrastination habit? How do we stop being a Procrastinator?

Well that is the very purpose of this habit changing handbook. Before you stop a bad habit, or replace a bad habit with a good one, you first need to understand what a habit is and how habits work. What feeds them, what allows them to happen, take root and take over your life?

The knowledge and understanding you get from this book, together with some honest self-assessment, some reflective thinking, a bit of simple task and time planning, together with spending a little time keeping a journal of your progress will have you stop procrastinating quickly and turn you from a prevaricator to being proactive in no time.

The Habit Changing Handbook

Appendix 3: Time management stops ticking

Why our time management stops ticking
(and what we can do about it)

Many of us appear to be obsessed time management –
probably because we never seem to have enough of it.
Despite using all those tools, apps on our smartphones and
computers, notebooks, journals, to-do lists with coloured
pens and other techniques, we sometimes find ourselves
spending more time on the time management system itself
than on doing the things we actually, should be doing
instead.

This can often lead to procrastination and can become a
vicious circle.

Some people have said that they try a new system, it works
for a while and then no longer works for them. They then look
for a time management system, and then another new shiny
app or journal that someone blogged about. There are just
so many resources, systems, tools and techniques, from
simple to-do lists on a sheet of paper to multi-level multi-user
cross operating system platforms with huge feature sets.

Time management systems can take over your life instead
of, as they so often promise, help you control your life.

It is a subject that is supported by a multitude of online
resources, countless blogs, guides and dedicated videos.
There are time management mentors and coaches, college,
university and training company courses all devoted to
helping you be better at managing your time. These
resources work for some people but not for others. They
work in some situations and not others. This can leave
people frustrated, anxious and even stressed – leading to
the opposite of effective productivity.

What makes so many people frustrated with time management?

Is there a better way of managing our time?

It has been said that "any system works so long as you work that system" so in the real world, when you boil it all down to the absolute basics, maybe it just comes down to our habits!

Productivity

Pursuing productivity for its own sake can be is counter-productive because of the self-imposed pressure we inflict upon ourselves and others with an ever-increasing list of things to do and dates to achieve them by. This may explain why we get so frustrated with time-management tools even to the point we just give up on them.
few weeks, they are more productive but still frustrated. "The real problem is that they are overworked, [it's] not a time-management problem."

The constant balancing act

Those of us working in factories, on production lines, don't seem to be worried about time management. We are told what to do and when, and we get paid for working to that recipe.

But so many of us now are becoming increasingly responsible for organising ourselves and being accountable to others for our time management and how we use our time productively.

That responsibility and accountability comes with a price – pressure to perform on time and to deadlines. Obviously then we need to really understand what makes us tick, what motivates us. By doing so we prevent that pressure from becoming stress.

The Habit Changing Handbook

There is no one-size solution

We are, for the most part, all individuals, all different, with different strengths and weakness, different desires, different levels of energy and enthusiasm – therefore a system that works for one of us will not work for another – there is no one-size-fits all solution to time management.

Many time management techniques evolved from the earlier days of manufacturing, as have many other management techniques. Time management is no different. Techniques and tools came about as solutions to particular problems someone else had which have been revised and adapted over time. Just web search "time management techniques" to find over 900 million results.

Taking control of your time to take control of your life

There are so many tools and techniques available at your disposal - to-do lists, calendars, timers, wallcharts, journals, apps, etc. This article is not about how to use those tools, our message here is that instead of using them to cramp your life with work, you should allow you to take control of your life, and then structure your work around it – not the other way around.

There is no holy grail (or is there?)

Life's big questions aside, is there a one-size-fits-all solution to stop procrastinating? Which are the best productivity and time management solutions for you?

An internet containing millions of videos, posts and pages promise an easy way to get things done.

Firstly, bear in mind that productivity is not an endless race, it's just a process for you to use and make it yours

Secondly, with so many to choose from it is worth spending time on research, consulting friends and colleagues and trying different tools and techniques for managing your time, procrastinating less and being more productive.

This would suggest there is no holy grail to stop your procrastination.

But maybe there really is one...... Habit!

At the end of the day it's your decision to change and it is your habits and behaviours which will make that decision work or not. By taking control of your habits you can make whatever systems and processes you adopt, work for you.

So instead of being a victim of your time management (or lack of), procrastinating habits, re-engineer your time management – replace your procrastinating putting-stuff-off habits with positive, productive, effective, time-managing, getting-stuff-done habits that will help you get to who and where you want to be.

At the end of the day - that's your holy grail!

The Habit Changing Handbook

Appendix 4. Time Management & Productivity Habits

"Don't say you don't have enough time. You have exactly the same number of hours per day that were given to Pasteur, Michelangelo, Mother Teresa, Leonardo da Vinci, Thomas Jefferson, Albert Einstein, Winston Churchill and Stephen Hawking." The question therefore is how are you spending your hours?

The point therefore is that we all have the same amount of time each day, it's just down to how well we manage and use it.

"Being busy" is not the same as managing your time properly – the old saying "work smarter, not harder" should come in to play when looking at how you spend your time.

There are thousands of articles on the internet about time management from which we have gleaned this list of good sensible advice habits

Complete most important tasks first.

This is one of the golden rules of a good time management habit. Every day identify a handful of tasks or activities that you really want to do, the most crucial to complete that day and do those first.

Once you've completed the first one, congratulate yourself and move on to the next. Once these essential tasks have been completed then you can move on to other things, or you postpone non-essential tasks until the next day.

Learn to say "no".

Saying yes and committing yourself soon helps you realise that you need to start juggling those commitments, and you need to start managing your time – which is good. However, sometimes things can get a little out of hand and you can so easily start to feel under pressure, which can lead to stress and suddenly you are on a downward spiral.

The solution is to, at some point, just say "not yet", or even a straight "no".

As soon as you learn this lesson, you should then be to take on only those commitments that you know you have time for and that you truly want to do.

Get enough sleep

Some of us believe that sacrificing sleep is a good way to hack productivity and get those extra working hours out of the working day.

Big mistake!

Most people need 7-8 hours of sleep for their bodies and minds to function optimally. You know if you're getting enough. Listen to your body, and don't underestimate the value of sleep.

Don't multi-task

Instead of trying to do too many things at the same, multi-tasking, maybe you should devote your entire focus concentration to the task at hand. Put away your distractions, turn off your notifications, put your phone out of sight and only use it for calls that can't wait.

The Habit Changing Handbook

Concentrate on this one task. Nothing else should exist. Immerse yourself in it.

Take over your environment

It's good to have a place to work that is quiet, and maybe listen to some music or even background noise. Some people like white or pink noise in the background, others like to use one of the several web apps online to play sounds on a long loop, such as wind, rain, waves, even the background noise of a coffee lounge.

Get started early.

We are nearly all plagued by the impulse to put things off, to procrastinate. It seems so easy just to do something else first, what's the harm? Many people who prefer to "be on top of things" and "ahead of the game", realise, the sooner you get it started, the sooner it will be completed and so you can get on with the next thing or reward yourself with a break.

The "devil is in the detail"

Tasks and projects often take much longer than they need to because one can get hung up on the small details.

A good saying is "Don't let perfection get in the way of completion." i.e. we can keep procrastinating by concentrating too much time on unimportant details.

Surely it is better to get the job done to a satisfactory standard to "get the job done" and if it needs to be refined then you can go back into the task and do so.

Turn your regular tasks into habits.

Many of us have regular tasks that need doing, daily, weekly monthly etc. How many of these tasks are scheduled – actually in the calendar. By making these regular tasks part of your schedule, you soon develop the habit to get them completed when they are supposed to be, done, out of the way, and not something that you have to build up to.

Be mindful of binge browsing, viewing and gaming

Time spent browsing social media, or binge watching box sets, on game consoles, and smart devices can be a huge drain on how productive you are, often because these things are so much more enjoyable than the jobs you need to do, which then stack up and become a small mountain to climb when you eventually get round to getting started.

You have 168 hours in a week – how about a fair split of a third of each week, 56 hours per week allocated for each of the following:

1. Downtime, sleeping and resting
2. Play, entertainment, socializing (online and in person)
3. Working and continuous professional development

That seems like a fair way to balance your week. However, these 'thirds' can be weighted as you see fit... Only want to spend 40 hours actually working, being productive, getting things done? Then that leaves you 128 hours. Take off your 8 hours a day recommended sleep and that leaves you 72 hours for yourself

Why not do a simple time audit over the next few weeks to understand how your time is being spent, well or otherwise?

Give yourself time limits and buffer breaks for tasks

Instead of sitting down to complete a marathon eight-hour session so that you can catch up, why not give yourself time slots, or zones, during the day to get tasks done. It is so important for heath and wellbeing to take breaks. Often by just banging your head against a task until its done, to the expense of other things, is not the answer.

When we have the habit of rushing from one task to the next and then the next it can be difficult to appreciate how well we are doing, to take stock, concentrate, focus and remain motivated.

Allowing ourselves breaks between tasks gives our brains a break too. Some people take a time out to grab a coffee, go for a walk, check the news, even meditate and be mindful for a few minutes.

Don't make you to-do list your enemy.

One of the fastest ways to drown in a sea of not getting stuff done when it needs to be is to look up at your mountainous wave of a to-do list. It is simply a series of bad habits that can cause this to happen. Developing a series of good time management habits made up of goals and rewards, scheduling, dealing with tasks in order of priority, not putting them off is one of the secrets of a good time management habit.

Sleep, rest, exercise lead a healthy lifestyle.

Many people still think that time management is all about work and productivity – this is so far from the truth of the matter. A good time management habit is about managing all of your time, and yourself.

Numerous clinical and productivity studies link wellbeing, mindfulness and a healthy lifestyle with personal productivity and happiness. Good time management habits enable you to deal with everyday pressures, both work wise and personally, and prevent those pressures from becoming stress.

Doing less not more.

This may sound counter intuitive but by doing less, by dealing with the more important things first instead of as they happen is a tactic favored by many people. Only commit to what you have time to do, things that matter and have value - nothing more.

Time management includes weekends too.

Many of us choose to work a little bit at the weekends for different reasons. There may be less interruptions, there is more quiet time, less distractions, more time to reflect. One reads of successful people who take time out of their Sunday afternoons to plan the week ahead. There are some who choose to work a little at the weekend using downtime, in order to give themselves more time during the week for different activities.

Just take time to get and stay organised

Being organised is a huge time-saver, and it need not be complicated. Unless of course you are a time-wasting procrastinator and spend your time management your time management system instead of actually getting things done.

Being organised is a great habit to have. It may mean having to file documents and files away where you can quickly locate them but that habit, that investment of time as you go along pays dividends quickly when it comes to getting things done.

Are you one of those people that fills the desk-top on your PC with random files, or just drops everything in to your 'my documents' folder? Your filing cabinet is that pile of bulging papers and envelopes stuffed onto and down the side of your bookshelf? How much time do you then waste looking for information, finding stuff, answering questions, etc.

To start a good time management habit, set some time aside to get organised and schedule in your calendar, 'admin days' to stay on top of things.

Don't sit around waiting.

OK, it's nice to switch off sometimes and do absolutely nothing. However, how much time do we waste waiting around, waiting for something to happen, waiting for someone else. Do something during waiting time.

Could that time we spend commuting, sitting in reception, waiting for a movie to download, etc. If you are not enjoying a bit of a mindful 'time out' stop waiting around, do something, whether its work, reading, listening to music or checking social media, that's all OK just don't waste time doing nothing at all.

Go into lockdown.

Sometimes, to really get things done you need to manage your time to do so. Set yourself a block of time exclusively for you to:

- shut yourself in to your space,
- shut yourself off from distractions,
- shut yourself out of social media and TV – no distractions, no interruptions, from anything or anyone that can prevent you from what you have set aside that time for.

Make a decision and schedule it.

A key part of good time management habits is to make a decision, commit to it and make an appointment with that commitment in your calendar. It doesn't matter if it's a work meeting, or a project that you need to finish, a session at the gym, or a social engagement. The message is simply deciding what you want to do, put it in your calendar, don't let anything else book that space and just do it.

Bin the non-essentials.

Ask yourself the following questions as part of your time management habit.
- How important is this, does it really need to be done, if so when shall I do it.
- How valuable is this – what difference will it make to me.
- Is what I am doing right now conducive to who I want to be, what I want to achieve and where I want to go? If not – why am I doing it?
- Am I procrastinating?

If it's not that important and doesn't really need to be done and its not letting anyone else down, just sack it. Give yourself more quality time

"Any system works so long as you work that system"

Time management is just a habit. Like any habit it can be good or bad. Good time management habits are positive, constructive and helpful. Therefore, identify what feeds your bad habits and replace them with helpful positive building new habits that will be to your advantage.

As you will have heard many times before, time is our most expensive commodity, once spent it can never be replenished.

Appendix 5. The Habit Changer on-line

Website

Discover more about what we do on our website:

http://habitchanger.co.uk

Facebook

Connect with us on Facebook:

https://www.facebook.com/abt.habit.journal

You can join our Facebook Community:

https://www.facebook.com/changing.habits.community

Instagram

Follow us on Instagram:

https://www.instagram.com/habit.changer

Twitter

Follow us on Twitter:

https://twitter.com/HabitJournal

Appendix 6: The Habit Changing Handbook Series

The easy read guides to changing your habits…

> … Permanently

> … and Stop Procrastinating

> … for Better Time Management

> … for Working from Home

> … around Weight Loss

The Habit Changing Handbook

Printed in Great Britain
by Amazon